2/-

Topside

OR

THE FUTURE OF
ENGLAND

He trespasses against his duty
who sleeps upon his watch,
as well as he
that goes over to the enemy.

—Burke

J. B. PRIESTLEY

Topside

OR

THE FUTURE OF ENGLAND

A DIALOGUE

HEINEMANN

LONDON   MELBOURNE   TORONTO

William Heinemann Ltd

LONDON   MELBOURNE   TORONTO
CAPE TOWN   AUCKLAND
THE HAGUE

First published 1958

© by J. B. PRIESTLEY 1958
All rights reserved

Printed in Great Britain
at The Windmill Press
Kingswood, Surrey

TOPSIDE

An elderly man, Jordan, has been giving dinner to a young man, Nigel, and now they are sitting over their coffee and brandy in Jordan's study.

JORDAN

Will you have a cigar?

NIGEL

No, thank you, sir. I don't smoke.

JORDAN

Sometimes I wish I didn't. We old smokers, trapped in our habit, are at the mercy of the Treasury, which has none. By the way, I forgot to ask about your Uncle Paul, Nigel. How is he, these days?

NIGEL

He's in great form. And just as pleased as Mother is about my getting into the Foreign Office. It was his idea originally. Following his footsteps sort of thing. Ever since Father died, Uncle Paul's kept an eye on me—been very decent really.

JORDAN

I'm sure he has. Remember me to him. He's spent so much time out of England that we've rarely seen each other, but we've been well acquainted ever since we were freshmen together at Cambridge. He's retired now, isn't he?

NIGEL

He's out of the Foreign service—yes. But—and this is rather confidential, as it hasn't been announced—he's being made director of this new institute that's being set up— *Culture In Industry*.

JORDAN

Is he indeed?

NIGEL

You sound rather surprised, Mr. Jordan.

JORDAN

I suppose I oughtn't to be. But after spending at least thirty years abroad in embassies, Paul can't have had much experience of culture in industry, if that means anything. And if it doesn't mean anything—which I suspect—then why have an institute of it?

NIGEL

Well, I'm very vague about it myself. But whatever it is, you obviously need the right kind of man to look after it. And I suppose that's where somebody like Uncle Paul comes in.

JORDAN

Yes, I'm sure it is, Nigel.

NIGEL

We had a long talk the other night about this very thing. Uncle Paul had taken me to Claridges to celebrate, after I'd heard I'd been accepted by the F.O. It was then he told me he was being given this new institute.

JORDAN

I'm probably jealous. Nobody offers me an institute—not even half of one.

NIGEL

Uncle Paul was telling me that from now on, whatever government might be in power, men with the right background and necessary experience could be certain of good administrative jobs, in or out of government service. The whole trend, he said, was in that direction.

JORDAN

He's quite right—it is.

NIGEL

Giving the country just the kind of stability it needs nowadays, he said. And I must say I couldn't agree more. Look at France.

JORDAN

I wish I could. I like looking at France, but at the moment I can't afford it, thanks to the high cost of stability here.

NIGEL

But we must have stability, don't you agree?

JORDAN

Not with any enthusiasm, Nigel.

NIGEL

But you agree with Uncle Paul?

JORDAN

I agree with him that the whole trend is in that direction.

NIGEL

And that it's a good thing?

JORDAN

No, not a very good thing. And part of a much worse
thing.

NIGEL

You're not serious, sir.

JORDAN

Yes, fairly, Nigel.

NIGEL

But what worse thing?

JORDAN

I call it Topside.

NIGEL

Topside?

JORDAN

Topside, Nigel. What are you grinning at?

NIGEL

It sounds like something you order from the butcher.

JORDAN

No, you can't eat Topside. Though perhaps it can eat you.

NIGEL

But what *is* it? What does it do?

JORDAN

Are you sure you want to know? It may take me some time to explain. I don't want to bore you, my boy.

NIGEL

I know you won't do that, Mr. Jordan. And I *do* want to know. So please go ahead.

JORDAN

We'll start at the hoardings. You must have noticed those *Times* advertisements—the paper read by Top People—or by those on their way to the Top?

NIGEL

Yes. Bit cheap, aren't they? Not quite *The Times* style, I'd have thought.

JORDAN

They're very revealing, in my opinion. Like a slip of the tongue. *The Times* might have said it was the paper read by intelligent people, or well-informed people, or cultivated people—and twenty years ago I think it would have said something of that sort—but now apparently it's enough to say that it's read by Top People. They may or may not be intelligent, well-informed, cultivated—we're not told—but what's certain is that they're at the Top, or on Top, or just Top. No other qualifying term necessary, it seems. A Top paper for Top people. Or, as I'd prefer to say, a Topside paper for Topside people, for Topsiders or would-be Topsiders.

NIGEL

Yes, but who are these Topside people, these Topsiders? Are you one?

JORDAN

No, Nigel. I'm an anti-Topside man.

NIGEL

Perhaps I am too.

JORDAN

No, I don't think so. You're headed for Topside. And I've no desire to convert you, my boy. I'm not a member of any party or movement. I'm no crusader. Just an old looker-on, that's all I am, Nigel. But of course a man can't help thinking, especially when he has as little to do as I have these days. And one of the things I keep thinking about is Topside.

NIGEL

But how would you describe it, sir? I seem to be for it, and you against it, but that's all I really know, so far. It's not a political party, I gather?

JORDAN

Oh—no. A Topsider might belong to either of the two big parties or to neither of them, to no political party, like a Civil Servant.

NIGEL

It's a social thing then, is it?

JORDAN

Partly, not entirely. It might be described as an interlocking power system. But that's perhaps too mechanical. It's more like an organism than a machine.

NIGEL

An organism?

JORDAN

A sort of gigantic human polyp. A Thing, but not from
outer space. It feeds on all the P's—power, place, privilege, patronage.

NIGEL

The establishment—sort of?

JORDAN

It's newer than the establishment and has replaced it. Just
as America now has Conformity to the Corporation, or
living in tune with General Motors, England now has
Topside. I say England, because I don't pretend to know
about Scotland, Wales, Northern Ireland. Moreover,
there are some peculiarly English elements in Topside.
Its use of tradition, for example.

NIGEL

I believe in that, Mr. Jordan. I mean, the way we like to
see things going on and on, changing them a little perhaps,
bringing them up-to-date, but keeping what's good in
them. That's what I like about England.

JORDAN

It's what you're intended to like.

NIGEL

And lots of people who come here admire it too. Several
Americans I know have told me.

JORDAN

It's one of the tourist attractions, I know. About thirty years ago I went to see the Passion Play at Ober-ammergau—simple pious villagers keeping up an old tradition. Only when I saw it, the Passion Play was being run by a travel agency. And English tradition is now being run by Topside.

NIGEL

I'm sorry—but I don't think I believe in this Topside.

JORDAN

Topside doesn't want you to believe in it. Topside hopes you think it isn't there. It's largely based on the enormous English capacity for self-deception. That's one reason why I limited myself to England—to leave out the Celts. A Celtic Topsider—and of course there are plenty of them—will deceive you but not himself: he knows what he's up to. But the English, in or out of Topside, can have a glorious time deceiving themselves about it.

NIGEL

But what's it supposed to do?

JORDAN

It takes and uses power, controls all patronage, imposes whatever pattern it prefers on the life of the nation.

NIGEL

But somebody has to run the country.

JORDAN

Quite so. But some of us like to see power divided and not

concentrated. It's also much healthier if different *kinds* of people take a hand in running the country, and without all this elaborate deception. And the wider and sharper the interest in how the country is being run, the better it is for everybody and for the country. That's the democratic idea. When it's actually put into practice, there's usually a great deal of argument, noise and confusion. Perhaps because it's alive. After all, happy families aren't the neatest and quietest. But anyhow we English are only democratic in theory. In practice we're now Topside.

NIGEL
But perhaps we prefer stability—balance——

JORDAN
A man might achieve stability and balance simply by having a ball and chain attached to each foot.

NIGEL
Surely you don't think this Topside of yours is like a ball and chain?

JORDAN
Oh, no. It's no obvious and brutal power system. In some ways it would be less dangerous if it were. It's a power system, certainly, but it maintains itself, constantly strengthening its position, by a series of conjuring tricks and illusions, appealing to the English capacity for self-deception.

NIGEL
In what way?

[9]

JORDAN

It never makes any appearance as itself. There are no Topside public relations and propaganda. It appears to represent almost everything except itself. Actually it stands for nothing except itself. Imagine in your house a monster polyp that you fed every day, watching it grow without any alarm, just because it was able to take on the appearance of a dachshund, two spaniel puppies, a basket of kittens, a cage of budgerigars, and bowls of goldfish. That's how Topside works. The large element of deceit is very important. Everything about Topside is a fake except its concealed possession and use of power. A good Topsider even deceives himself. He's the bit of the monster polyp that goes on barking like a dog or mewing like a kitten even when there's nobody in the room.

NIGEL

Easy on the science fiction, please, Mr. Jordan! And I must say that so far it seems to me you're only saying in effect that some people want to govern just as a lot of others simply want to be governed. And I think the people who really care about this country and who want to serve it are part of what you call Topside. And I say *Good luck to 'em!* And if that makes me a Topsider, I'm delighted.

JORDAN

Yes, but remember, you don't know all about Topside yet, far from it. But go on.

NIGEL

I admit I don't understand yet what you mean by this elaborate deception business—perhaps you can give me some examples later——

JORDAN

I can—and it won't be possible to stop me——

NIGEL

But I'd like to say this. Though most of your Topsiders
may belong to a certain class and may have been educated
at public schools and the older universities, I don't believe
—whatever you may say, Mr. Jordan—that Topside is a
class thing.

JORDAN

Neither do I.

NIGEL

Oh—don't you? Somehow you sounded as if you did.

JORDAN

No, this isn't our old acquaintance—the class system. It's
much newer and a great deal more subtle than that.

NIGEL

Anyhow, what I believe is that your Topside people are
simply those who want to use their brains in the service of
their country, who aren't afraid of responsibility, who don't
think in terms of hours and wages and amusement, and
who, if they do belong to a new ruling class, are the only
people fit to belong to it. Somebody has to run the country,
and if the Topsiders don't do it, who will?

JORDAN

A great many people who aren't Topsiders, Nigel, and
never could be. But go on.

B

NIGEL

If what you call Topside were barring useful people because they hadn't the right background, that would be something else——

JORDAN

No, it's foreground rather than background that matters——

NIGEL

Well, I take it that anybody who has the necessary ability and the right attitude of mind can become a Topsider?

JORDAN

With any luck—yes, Nigel.

NIGEL

And there have to be Topsiders. There always have been. And now that we've fifty million people who expect a high standard of living, plenty of amusement, a state organised to take care of them, and who at the same time don't want to think for themselves, what you call Topside's more necessary than ever before. So I'm not going to attack Topside. I'm all for it. And I can't see why you aren't, Mr. Jordan.

JORDAN

Because you've missed the point or I haven't succeeded yet in making it. To begin with, I thought I'd made it clear that Topside isn't a new name for something that's gone on a long time. It's a new name because it's describing something new. It wasn't in existence before the war or during it. But I suspect that Stanley Baldwin, in his own rather subtle and intuitive fashion, caught an approaching whiff of Topside. This was after the ignominious collapse of Ramsay MacDonald's Labour Government in 1931. Topside was stirring then in the womb of Time. MacDonald himself, after he formed the National Government, backed by Baldwin and the Tories, was a kind of early prototype Topsider. He represented everything and stood for nothing, except remaining in Downing Street. Beautiful primitive Topsiding. The speeches he made—I heard several of them—were nonsense because they obviously didn't refer to any recognisable reality. Crude and early Topsiding, of course. In the end he thinned out and dwindled to a mere ghostly appearance. But then there was no Topside to nourish him. Pre-war Toryism wasn't Topside but simply its own stupid self, if we except some earlier intuitive Topside flashes from Baldwin, who incidentally, by defeating Edward VIII, made it easy for Topside later to take over the Crown. But first, there had to be the war, which was the opposite of Topside——

NIGEL

Sorry to butt in—but what exactly do you mean by that?

JORDAN

In a war, Nigel, the English stop deceiving themselves. It's too dangerous. Appearance and reality have to be made to fit—or it's all up. Everything has to be real, sooner or later, or the war's lost. Soldiers have to be soldiers, generals to be generals. The munition makers must produce munitions; the aircraft manufacturer must really manufacture aircraft, which is something quite unnecessary, as we've learnt at some cost, in peace-time. And anybody will do for any job, no matter how eccentric and unsound and far from being the right type he is, so long as he can really do it. I assure you that if we were plunged into the same kind of war as the last one, Topside would vanish in a few weeks. But unfortunately for England, we've arranged that if there should be another war then we'll all be obliterated long before we can rid ourselves of Topside, which indeed might outlast most of us. I don't think this explains why Topside's so strongly in favour of nuclear weapons, though it's a thought.

NIGEL

Topside, then, came into existence after the war. But when? During the Labour Government?

JORDAN

It's hard to say exactly when it began. It's quietly grown, getting bigger and stronger and more sure of itself all the time. But nobody plotted and planned it into existence. That's not how these things happen, at least not in England. Rational and radical thinkers are always too apt to assume that the people on the other side know exactly what they're doing, that they make plans and carry them out, all in the full light of consciousness. This is quite wrong. The kind of men who make good Topsiders hardly let themselves know what they're up to; they never discover their motives, let alone discuss them; they move unconsciously and instinctively into defensive and offensive alliances; and they can all sit round a table, kick one fellow out of a job, hoist another fellow into it, all without ever finding any real reasons for what they're doing. But if I can't tell you exactly when Topside came into existence, I can tell you *why* it did, Nigel. *Topside's the reaction against a revolution that never happened.*

[14]

NIGEL

I thought we were supposed to have had one, just after the war.

JORDAN

No, that's the one that never happened. It lived long enough to put Attlée in, and then died. Some think it was suicide; I say it was murder. One day in the late summer of '45, Revolutionary Young England was invited to 10 Downing Street, to be thanked for its election services, and was shot as it went upstairs. Who pulled the trigger, I don't know. Incidentally, there's an excellent photograph in the paper today of Earl Attlee sweating away in his uniform of a Knight of the Garter. But though the revolution never quite happened, the reaction did.

NIGEL

I wonder. Perhaps it's a reaction that never happened against a revolution that never happened. Perhaps you can't tell me when Topside came into existence because it never did. I'll tell you frankly, sir, I don't believe it exists outside your imagination.

JORDAN

In a sense you're right, Nigel. Topside's in my mind and nowhere else. But the something to which I give the name Topside—*that* exists——

NIGEL

But as what? It isn't a party; it isn't an organisation; it isn't even a class. Or is it? I don't mean a social class but a new and rather streamlined up-to-date ruling class. Because if that's it, I'm all for it. I hope you're right, and that it does exist. You said either I'd missed the point or you hadn't made it. Well, sir, it seems to me you still haven't made it. And even if you convince me that Topside really exists, I'll still be all for it.

JORDAN

Even if you thought it would ruin this country?

NIGEL

No, of course not, but why should it?

JORDAN

We'll come to that. But let's take a look at the country first. There in the middle, a central citadel of power, I see Topside. All round it, stretching as far as the eye can see, are what we could call the Takers. They represent the bulk of the English people, mostly belonging to what used to be called the working class. In spite of inflation, most of these people, the Takers, unlike their fathers and mothers, aren't dissatisfied with their lot. All burning sense of social injustice has vanished——

NIGEL

I should think so.

JORDAN

No dream of anything much better disturbs them. Mass amusements keep boredom at bay. Not completely perhaps because now and again many of them must feel that something's missing, and this occasional feeling of frustration probably explains some odd explosions of resentment and violence. But when their Prime Minister tells them they've "never had it so good", they can't disagree, even if they don't agree with any enthusiasm. But then, away from the football stands, they don't show any enthusiasm. They're not on the whole politically-minded nor public-spirited, but they're still fairly responsive to traditional appeals to them as decent citizens. And I think that's a fair if sketchy picture of the Takers.

NIGEL

Yes, but why do you call them Takers?

JORDAN

To indicate their relation to Topside. They take what Topside offers them. And now we can see a ring of people between Topside and the Takers, and these people are quite different. They're not Topsiders and don't want to be Topsiders, and they're equally not Takers.

NIGEL

Ah—you like these people, Mr. Jordan. I can hear it in your voice.

JORDAN

Certainly I do. I'm one of them. Now politically they can only belong to the extremes of the two big parties, which are themselves Topside. Or they may be anarchists, rebellious radicals, saints, philosophers, crackpots. Where they differ from both Topsiders and Takers is that they can't be satisfied with appearance at odds with reality, they're suspicious of disguises and illusions and conjuring tricks, they don't like familiar and comfortable phrases that have lost all real meaning. And—this is important—*they believe in something*.

NIGEL

But don't Topsiders?

JORDAN

Certainly not. I thought I'd made that clear, my boy. A good Topsider believes in nothing except being at or on the Top.

NIGEL

Oh—that's rather sweeping, isn't it? After all, I suppose you'd call Uncle Paul a Topsider, wouldn't you?

JORDAN

I would.

NIGEL

Well, he believes in something.

JORDAN

Does he? In what?

NIGEL

Well—offhand I can't say——

JORDAN

Then allow me to continue. These non-Takers, these rebels, these anti-Topsiders, may believe in very different things. They may believe in the infallibility of the Pope or in the *Anima Mundi*. They may believe that England should be governed by commissars or country gentlemen. They may believe we should spend every pound we can possibly spare on opera houses, theatres, art galleries, or that we shouldn't give them a penny and pull down the few we have as soon as we can. But they believe in *something*. And so they can see through Topside. They know it doesn't stand for anything except itself. They know its religion isn't religious but merely respectable, that its royalty isn't kingly, its patriotism has no love of country, its politics is a mere power game, its journalism a constant tampering with the truth.

NIGEL

In other words, they're Topside's opposition. And this country doesn't mind oppositions. It's the basis of our system, to accept the opposition as such. That's what so many foreigners can't understand—that in the House we can have an official and salaried leader of Her Majesty's Opposition.

JORDAN

My dear boy, that's merely a cosy Topside arrangement. A real opposition—genuinely hostile, jeering and denouncing—receives very different treatment, and with the approval of both sides of the House. I've told you that among other things Topside's a defensive and offensive alliance. Or even a kind of organism. Challenge it and it strikes back. And what's happening now is that this ring of non-Takers, anti-Topsiders, is becoming narrower and narrower and may soon be squeezed out of existence. In a few years any rebellious, radical, nonconforming type may be faced with the choice of turning Topsider or disappearing into the vast outer ring of Takers.

NIGEL

I don't see that. Why should he? Don't tell me that in a few years we'll all have the secret police watching us— 1984 stuff.

JORDAN

No, I wasn't thinking about secret police.

NIGEL

Then what's to stop the rebel from going on being rebellious?

JORDAN

Nothing. But he won't be able to tell a lot of other people why he's rebellious. He won't have a platform.

NIGEL

Why not? Who'll take it away from him?

JORDAN

Topside. It's doing that already. It controls more and more channels of communication, monopolises more and more platforms. The air may not be completely controlled by Topside yet, but it's harder and harder for a critic of Topside to get much time on the air, easily his best way of reaching the Takers. There are still a few newspapers that don't take orders from Topside or, what amounts to the same thing, don't have Topside proprietors and editors. But only a few. And rebels against Topside aren't going to be able to collect several million pounds to start a newspaper of their own. Then most periodicals and all popular magazines take care not to challenge Topside. If I wrote down what I'm saying to you tonight, no popular magazine would print it. We don't have a censorship of the press in this country. We've something much more effective—Topside proprietors and plenty of managing editors and feature editors who know how their bread's buttered.

We've also just had some Angry Young Men who've been given plenty of publicity and have done very nicely out of rebellion. And what's happened to them seems to me to wreck your argument.

Not at all. It might if these young men had been really rebelling, putting dangerous ideas into people's heads, telling them what to hit and how to hit it. But they've only been letting steam off, pretending to rebel. If any of these boys stop merely letting steam off and begin to hit where it hurts, you'll find they'll not do as well as they've been doing. There's even a Topside book world now, with Topsider critics and reviewers hard at work, building up reputations to win Topside literary prizes. And as for letting steam off, pretending to rebel, Topside doesn't mind that, welcomes it. Some of the most effective and useful Topsiders are the imitation rebels. They'll provide you for nothing with much better character acting than you pay a pound to see in discomfort at the theatre. *My God—how right you are, old boy!* they tell you, over expense-sheet double Scotches or giant gins and tonics. *How much longer are we going to put up with these types? Boot 'em all out, I say! What about the other half?* Sometimes I wonder if Topside's running a school of acting somewhere. These rough tough fellows, so different from the usual Topside smoothies, used to take me in every time, right up to the moment when the knife was in the back. But not any more, Nigel. And if you're determined to settle in Topside, then look out for the imitation rebels, who probably do their stuff to test fellow Topsiders as well as to deceive genuine rebels. Meanwhile, sooner or later, these people who do believe in something, who can't accept appearance as reality, who know that Topside's a vast fake, will be muzzled or gagged. That'll leave Topside and the Takers, the bulk of the English, together without any interruptions, on a permanent honeymoon.

NIGEL

I hope you're right. Those who want to govern are left with all those who want to be governed. What's wrong with that?

JORDAN

Everything.

NIGEL

It seems to me a lot of time, energy and fuss would be saved, and that very soon the country would be a good deal better off than it is now. But of course you don't agree.

JORDAN

To show you how much I disagree, Nigel, I'll tell you this. We've only to have a completely confident and impregnable Topside, surrounded by an uncritical and docile people, to begin the ruin of England——

NIGEL

Now, really, Mr. Jordan—that's a bit much——

JORDAN

I tell you, between them they would turn this country into a depressed area, an unending slum, the neglected grave of a great nation.

NIGEL

Oh—rubbish! I'm sorry—but that really is rubbish.

JORDAN

Don't apologise—just tell me why you think it's rubbish.

NIGEL

Well, I can't see you've got the slightest excuse for saying what you did. It doesn't begin to make sense to me. Look here—we'd have stability—good government—sound administration—and people of every class working at the jobs they're fit to do. And all that can bring prosperity. What we *wouldn't* have is the very thing that can't bring prosperity—argument, useless criticism, silly revolutionary talk, radical objections to everything and everybody, all that sort of thing. And I'll tell you frankly, Mr. Jordan, I don't care if what you call the platform for this kind of stuff disappears for ever. The sooner it goes, the better. I think one sound hard-working administrator is more real use to the country than all your radicals, non-conformers, rebels, put together. And if that makes me a Topsider, I'm proud to be one.

JORDAN

The ruin of England, my dear Nigel.

NIGEL

I can't believe you're serious, sir.

JORDAN

Indeed I am. And Topside could probably do it in ten years. I don't expect to see it, but you will.

NIGEL

Well, we seem to have reached a deadlock. You think—
and I can't imagine why—that Topside can ruin England.
I think only what you call Topside can keep England
going. So where do we go from here?

JORDAN

In the direction, I hope, of a few points I still have to make.
You can't imagine how Topside could ruin England, so
you must allow me to tell you. Now let's begin with your
little Topside manifesto, about the importance of stability,
good government, sound administration, people working
at the jobs they're fit for, and so forth. Now of course
stability's important——

NIGEL

I should think so.

JORDAN

But not in England, Nigel. If I lived, say, in Guatemala,
I'd probably be demanding stability at almost any price.
But not in England. There seems to me a great deal of
stability in the English, and if Topside's busy adding more
stability, increasing the weight, so to speak, isn't there a
danger that soon there might be too much stability? Most
of the English I know aren't suffering from instability.
Nor is English life. I never find myself wondering when
this life and these people will begin at last to settle down,
when they'll stop imitating kaleidoscopes and firework
displays, when they'll put bridle and bit on the fiery steeds
of their imagination and passions. Visitors from abroad
never condemn our whirligig existence here, our gay idle
sensuality. They used to in the sixteenth century, but they

haven't now for some time. Our manufacturers and exporters aren't asked by their customers abroad to be steadier and less brilliantly experimental. Our political and official circles aren't notorious for their fantastic brawling or the wit and fancy of their talk. I'm still a member of several clubs, and I never catch a glimpse of one of them that suggests that ours is a feverishly unstable society. At times abroad I've seen men working with a wild energy that seemed almost out of control, but here in England there usually seems far more control than energy. If Topside has plans to increase the stability of the English, it might also seriously consider sending sand to the Sahara and ice to the Antarctic. But I doubt if it has. As I've suggested before, Nigel, Topside stands for nothing but itself, and the only stability it's worried about is its own. And there you needn't worry. Topside has plenty of stability.

NIGEL

I'm glad you think so, Mr. Jordan. Suits me.

JORDAN

Quite so. But I hope you'll agree now that the stability argument in favour of Topside won't do. It's not stability but something quite different that the English need, and now we must see what Topside has to offer. We've agreed that able men aren't barred from Topside because of their social background and lack of public school and older university education. To criticise Topside on an Old School Tie basis is stupid.

NIGEL

You're dead right, of course. Though I'm surprised to hear you say so.

JORDAN

Then, my boy—and now I must be severe with you—
either you've not been listening or you've not taken in
what I've said. I'd hoped I'd made it quite clear that Topside couldn't possibly be governed by old-fashioned social
snobbery. If it were, it would have to believe in something—no matter how stupid—outside itself. But I
maintain it believes in nothing outside itself. And unless
you grasp this, you can't follow my argument. This lack
of any belief is its immediate strength but will soon prove
to be a fatal weakness. For men have to believe in something outside themselves to be genuinely creative; and
shortly I'll return to this point. But we've agreed that
Topside has no social and educational tests for prospective
Topsiders. In fact it's ready to welcome some straight-
from-the-people-and-no-bloody-nonsense chaps, the Eds
and Teds; for some of them make first-class imitation
rebels. All Topside demands of them is that they don't
believe in anything except being at the Top. And it's this
that gives Topside its apparent strength and stability.
Now after stability, you mentioned good government, I
think.

NIGEL

Yes, I did. I'm sure that any government with Topside
behind it is more sure of itself and more likely to be a good
government. Governments have to be able to govern.
We've seen what happened in France.

JORDAN

We've also seen what happened in England. After Suez,
for instance.

NIGEL

Oh dear!

JORDAN

Quite so. *Suez!* An action decided upon, without any reference to the feelings and wishes of the nation, by a tiny group of ministers secretly supported by a few important non-political Topsiders. An episode possibly unique in modern British history because, no matter from what point of view it's regarded, it appears equally idiotic and disastrous. No enemy of Britain is clever enough to have designed for her such a supreme piece of imbecility. Even Topside, hurrying to its defence, hardly knew what to say or how to say it. But what happened afterwards? It was then that the new England of these 'Fifties, Takers controlled by Topside, fully revealed itself. It was then I realised I was living in a different country. For after Suez, nothing happened.

NIGEL

Except that Eden, a sick man, resigned, and Macmillan took over.

JORDAN

Yes, but the whole sick government ought to have resigned. And in your father's time—and most certainly in *my* father's time—there'd have been such an outcry that the government would have fallen like coal down a chute. But all we were expected to do was to keep quiet and foot the bill. This was the new Topside England with everything nicely under control. As you say, Harold Macmillan took over. Himself a Suez man, unrepentant and bland, he quite coolly took over. And I may be doing him an injustice, but I can't help feeling that, anxious though he may be at times to please Taker televiewers, there is about him a faint suggestion of swagger and insolence, an undercurrent of contemptuous amusement in that drawl of his; as if somebody had told him his brain was showing, and he just didn't care. So later if his Chancellor of the Exchequer resigns, he doesn't postpone the flight round the Commonwealth he proposes to enjoy. Why should he? Political crises are old stuff, out of date; he's no fool; he knows where he's living now, in new Topside England.

NIGEL

But suppose, after the next general election, he's out and Gaitskell's in?

JORDAN

It'll still be Topside England. Topsiders holding key posts won't be removed to make room for anti-Topsiders. Rebels against Topside won't have an inch more platform than they have now. The narrowing and squeezing out of nonconformity won't be stopped. Official Labour won't do anything about Topside. Once you accept without question all the Topside arrangements, from the control of mass communications to the Changing of the Guard, you've delivered yourself to Topside. You know, Keir Hardie was the first Labour member, and it's said he arrived at the House wearing a cloth cap. Labour should have kept to that cloth cap.

NIGEL

Oh—come, Mr. Jordan! Does it matter what a man wears?

JORDAN

If it doesn't, then why go to the trouble and expense of acquiring top hats, morning coats, court suits?

NIGEL

Because on certain occasions it's customary to wear such things——

JORDAN

But that's accepting somebody else's tradition, becoming a customary party. When Labour came into power, it should have said: "That may be your tradition but it isn't ours. Our traditional costume is a blue serge lounge suit and a cloth cap. Like it or lump it!"

NIGEL

You're not serious now.

JORDAN

I'm making the point that once you've accepted part of a tradition, it's impossible to take drastic action against the whole of it. A Keir Hardie in a cloth cap feels himself free to change society from top to bottom. A Ramsay Mac-Donald, enjoying himself in knee-breeches and silk stockings, doesn't feel himself free to do anything, except to change into some other fancy dress. A Labour leader in silk stockings is a contradiction. If the silk stockings are essential, then Labour isn't. If Labour means what it says, then the silk stockings are out. Remember that Labour began as a movement to change society, and not to keep the same play and costumes and merely change the cast. It was returned in '45 as a revolutionary movement. But when it came in, it accepted too much, accepted everything except the bow of burning gold and arrows of desire it had been asking for at all meetings accompanied by an organ. It did just enough to create a reaction, to bring Topside into existence. Any dragon's teeth it insisted upon sowing merely produced more and more new bowler hats and brief-cases. Unless very strange things happen, the next Labour Government will be almost as much a Government under Topside as our present one is. Few if any Topside controls will be disturbed. Its key appointments will be left alone. Topside can be happy with Gaitskell. It's my guess that like almost all English politicians now, Left or Right, he shares with Topside the administration fallacy.

NIGEL

Is there one? If so, what is it?

JORDAN

Well, Nigel, as you seem to share it too, you'd better understand what it is. Remember, you put a lot of emphasis upon sound administration, and said that one sound hard-working administrator was worth all my radicals, nonconformers, rebels, put together?

NIGEL

I'll stand by that. What's the fallacy?

JORDAN

The idea that administration is the most important thing there is. Which in turn means that the head man in any enterprise must be an administrator. Or that your Uncle Paul should be put in charge of Culture In Industry. It's this idea—setting aside your Uncle Paul—that makes Topside so dangerous. This is one reason—there are others—

why it could ruin England. You see, Nigel, behind all very successful enterprises that have brought something new and valuable into the world, from cars and aircraft to opera and theatre companies, you'll always find a certain kind of man, and I can assure you he's never an administrator. Topside wouldn't want him, and he wouldn't want Topside. He's an originating, innovating, creative type, entirely different from the administrative type in temperament, outlook, and even in the way he uses his energy. He's a man who has a passion for what he's doing, believes he can create something new and better, and by energy, enthusiasm, will, he's able to coax, persuade, bully and drive a lot of other people to help him. And in the end, often against heavy odds, he *makes* something, for he's essentially a *maker*. Now this kind of man is equally indispensable in the arts, sciences, education, industry. Try to do without him, and stagnation sets in. And ordinary people, just Takers, in their intuitive way, recognise this innovating, originating, creative type, and though they may grumble about him, just because he sometimes drives them hard, they can't help responding to his enthusiasm, to his passionate concern for something outside himself, his vision of something new and better. Whenever skilled technicians and workmen are restive, bored, unwilling to give extra time to the job, you can bet they're out of contact with the creative man, who's probably just been replaced by a sound administrator. No matter how stupid, narrow, selfish, people may seem to be, most of them, perhaps all but the psychological misfits, want to be part of something greater than themselves. This is why real statesmen, unlike the common run of politicians, never appeal to the self-interest of their audiences; they compel their listeners to rise to another and nobler level of existence. And creative men have something of this effect. The people who work for and with them begin to live in their atmosphere. They catch fire from their courage and enthusiasm. And no matter how large new enterprises may become, they still owe everything to one or two exceptional men. Now, Nigel, do you agree that there are such men and that they are of very great value to any community?

NIGEL

Certainly I do.

JORDAN

Would you also agree that no country needs such men more urgently than England does? We have a lot of people, a high standard of living, few natural resources, and must make things that other countries want to buy. So we depend on our wits and inventiveness. Right?

NIGEL

Right. I agree with all this. But I don't see where Topside and the administration fallacy come in. There have to be administrators. And these creative men you've been talking about are obvious Topsiders.

JORDAN

No, Nigel, that's just what they're not. They can't be fitted into Topside. They mistrust it, and it mistrusts them. A creative man doesn't want to deceive himself or anybody else; he has to be concerned with reality and not with appearance; he has to believe in something outside himself. And all this is contrary to Topside. You'll remember I defined it as a power organism. It's a controller, not a maker. Naturally then, with Topside, administration comes first. The idea, which is now hardly challenged, that the controller is superior to the maker, the administrator to the originator, is essentially a Topside idea. All Topside appointments are made on this basis. And as Topside becomes more and more powerful, there'll be less and less scope for creators, originators, innovators, just because they're not Topsiders and can't help being opposed to the Topside idea. So with Topside triumphant, there's bound to be more and more control of less and less making. There'll be larger and larger brakes for a smaller and smaller engine. And remember, the platform of protest, criticism, challenge, is shrinking rapidly too. The very people who would always support the creative type, the very people who largely produce the type, are now in danger of being silenced. And while Topsiders can stop things being made, can maintain some sort of routine, they can't make anything new themselves any more than the brakes can propel the car.

NIGEL

But even if all this were true, you have only to enlarge Topside to include these originating characters——

JORDAN

But it can't include them unless it changes its whole nature, and of course it won't do that. Power systems never do. They can't enlarge themselves because there's nothing outside themselves they believe in that they can reach out to. They can be changed from the outside but not from the inside. And now, Nigel, I want to justify my remark, which you disagreed with so violently, that Topside can ruin England. For England, as you'll admit, is in a precarious position.

NIGEL

Yes. That's why I believe in the people who want to govern taking charge of the people who want to be governed, and in getting on with it without a lot of criticism and fuss and wild talk.

JORDAN

No doubt. But I'm afraid that's Topside stuff. There's more here than governing and being governed. A nation has to be thoroughly awake, alert, alive, to save itself and then improve its position in the world, and when it is alive, there's bound to be a lot of criticism and fuss and wild talk. The quietest people are the dead, the most docile the zombies. Now England needs two things to keep its place in the world and to avoid becoming one enormous depressed area. It needs ideas and energy. Boldly inventive new ideas and sufficient energy to make them into something. And we need more of these ideas than we have at present and a far greater release of energy. But Topside can't create the ideas and it can't release the energy. And that's not all; I wish it were. For in my opinion, Topside discourages such ideas and cuts down the supply of national energy.

NIGEL

Why should it be so stupid?

JORDAN

The danger of dealing in unreality, as Topside does, is that you may come to deceive yourself. Topsiders would indignantly deny that they were in any way opposed to men of ideas. I can hear them doing it. *I can assure you, Mr. Chairman sir, and you ladies and gentlemen, that my col-*

leagues and I will be only too delighted to give—er—the
warmest possible welcome to men of ideas. Any suggestion to
the contrary is a deliberate distortion of the facts. They may
even believe this, having begun to deceive themselves.
What they forget is that Topside has already decided in
favour of the decent sound administrator whose one idea is
to keep out of trouble. This is its man. Therefore it can't
welcome the opposing type, the creative man of ideas, who
probably won't be a decent sound fellow at all and will
make trouble all over the place. The truth is, you can't
have ideas on Topside terms. It's like asking for a fixed
routine and plenty of experiment at one and the same time.
Also, if Topside is doing everything it can to reduce the
area of nonconformity, criticism, rebellion, then it's reduc-
ing the very territory where ideas come from, the region
of bold free minds. So much for ideas.

NIGEL
All right. But what about this energy business? I take it
that if more energy is needed, it has to come from people
in general, your Takers. And as you say yourself that Topside has them well under control, why shouldn't it make
them more energetic?

JORDAN
Nobody can say Topside hasn't tried. It makes innumer-
able appeals, using every possible device, even dressing up
the Radio Doctor as Head of Propaganda and sending
Lord Hailsham on tour with his bell-ringing act. But the
people don't respond. They keep quiet. They don't use
their energy the wrong way, smashing things up. But no
enthusiasm can be generated in them, no energy freely
released. Why? Because simple people, not given to

using their intellects, tend to be intuitive. And on the deeper level where intuition works and where enthusiasm and new stores of energy could be found, Topside fails with them. It fails just because it doesn't believe in anything but itself. And intuition senses that. On that deeper level, Topside's illusions have no effect.

NIGEL

But you said that Topside controlled these people.

JORDAN

So it does, but control can't produce enthusiasm and energy. It can keep people quiet and more or less satisfied in a bewildered *Is-this-all-there-is?* fashion. It can offer them a series of shows to amuse them. But it can't reach that extra store of energy. For that you need belief responding to belief, as in 1940 when Churchill told them he was ready to fight to the last ditch. They responded with everything they had because they knew he meant what he said, just as later, when he spoke as a peace-time politician, they didn't respond on this deeper level because their intuition told them he was beginning to talk Topside stuff. To be really moved and not merely kept quiet, people have to be converted to a belief. But Topside has no belief to bring about this conversion. Except as a power, privilege, patronage system, which it must pretend not to be, it's just a colossal sham. The largest fake antique shop of all time. Its religion is government department religion, ready to accept anything, hydrogen bombs and all, if it seems like sound policy. Its loyalty to the Crown is all super-show business, not a genuine belief in monarchy. Its patriotism has so little pride that it allows a foreign army to be stationed here, accepts this country as somebody else's expendable rocket base, and can no longer imagine the English taking a line of their own. Its love of our national culture, our heritage of this and that, begins and ends with after-dinner speeches; while whole floors of museums and art galleries have been closed down so that we can afford to send more people to watch nuclear explosions, cultural organisations are being dunned out of existence by new demands for rates and taxes, and its civil list pensions are well below the price of mere existence. Its dignified journalism, so dignified that its staff assassins are all anonymous, no longer cares about telling its readers the truth but only about Topside policy. Compare it with similar journalism fifty or a hundred years ago, and see how evasive and slimy it's become. And out of this gigantic sham, in which nothing's real but the desire for power and place, privilege and patronage, how could anything emerge to win a response from the heart and the imagination of the people? I tell you, my boy, England will run down like an old clock that's had its winding key mislaid.

NIGEL

Then why isn't it doing that now? According to you, Mr. Jordan, Topside's already in full swing, and yet we're not doing so badly.

JORDAN

Because we're still living on a pre-Topside accumulation of belief and goodwill. Topside's not producing its maximum effect yet. Give it a little more time, and it will. Remember, it's trying hard to blanket and muffle all criticism. And it's busy encouraging the worst English vice— self-deception, and, for the time being, until the country starts running down, is flourishing on it. Its organisation, strategy and tactics are all designed to keep the English deceiving themselves. There'll soon be a special emigration plan for people suffering from intellectual honesty. Victims of integrity will either be operated on or sent round ringing a bell, like the old lepers.

NIGEL

I'll bet. And what do you propose to do about it all, Mr. Jordan?

JORDAN

If I'd my way—and I needn't give you the odds against my having my way—everything that Topside's supposed to stand for would be ruthlessly examined and then, most of it, shot at. Then Topside would either be compelled to believe in something or be shot to pieces. If it believed in something, then its character might change; and if it were shot to pieces, then at least we'd be rid of it.

NIGEL

What would you start on? Its religion?

JORDAN

Certainly. No more official Topside Church and churchmen. No more Topside administration preaching the gospel according to Pontius Pilate. No more archbishops and bishops arriving out of the Prime Minister's office. No more of this timid respectability, this uncharitable sexual prejudice, this blessing of anything sanctioned by official policy, masquerading as religion. Either the Church of England has some spiritual vitality or it hasn't. If it hasn't, let it wither away. If it has, then it ought to welcome disestablishment, that is, ridding itself of the establishment. And let it fight for itself with its own spiritual weapons, instead of calling in the armed forces, the police, the bailiffs. Let it beg for bread instead of foreclosing mortgages. And if every Topsider in ecclesiastical costume vanishes from the Church, so much the better. How can a genuine priest be a Topsider? Or be anything but dubious about rank and privilege? When I was a soldier in the First War, Nigel, I found that the men, who mostly hadn't any religion, greatly preferred the Catholic priests or the nonconformists to the C. of E. chaplains. This wasn't the fault of the official chaplains, who were often very good fellows, but of the system, which made them official, gave them uniforms and rank and the wrong kind of authority. Real religion and social status shouldn't be on speaking terms. And the people, in their intuitive way, feel that.

NIGEL

Steady now, Mr. Jordan! Aren't you contradicting yourself? First you say that Topside puts it over the people through religion, among other things, and now you're suggesting it doesn't.

JORDAN

No, Nigel, there's no real contradiction. Again, it's a question of two different levels. On the more superficial level, social and ceremonial, the Church is an effective Topside instrument. So the Archbishop of Canterbury is the stately and most imposing personage everybody saw on television, crowning the Queen. A big-wig, if there ever was one. That's the level on which Topside succeeds. But when we come to religion itself, we're down to another level, served by intuition, and on that level most of the English people, all the humble Takers, reject the Church just because they recognise it's Topside. If the Church suddenly denounced Topside from every pulpit, called down the wrath of God on men still ready to play power politics with hydrogen bombs, lashed out at all the lies and hypocrisies, challenged England to mend her ways or go screaming down to Hell, there'd be new converts by the million. But the Church, solidly set in Topside, can't and daren't; so cut it loose, I say; allow it to refresh itself spiritually in the official wilderness, where religion belongs.

NIGEL

And the Crown?

JORDAN

For the good of the country, it can't possibly stay as it is.

NIGEL

You realise that if you said that in public, within twenty-four hours you'd be the most unpopular man in the country?

JORDAN

No doubt I'd appear to be, Nigel. Topside and its press and that press's noisy lunatic fringe would see to that. Thanks to them, no public man these days dare announce that he's a republican, though as you must know there were plenty of declared republicans in public life before our time.

NIGEL

I also know that the most popular figures in England today are the members of the Royal Family.

JORDAN

You may be right, though not all the stories I hear, especially from the North, bear you out. To some people Topside's beginning to show through. Ah—I see you wince, my boy.

NIGEL

I don't want to be pompous about it, but I happen to believe in the Crown. And I also very much dislike the sort of stupid ill-natured personal criticisms of the Queen that——

JORDAN

No, no, Nigel, I'll respect your chivalrous feeling about these royal ladies, so handsome and yet so dutiful. Though a Roundhead rather than a Cavalier myself, I think they perform a particularly tedious series of tasks—for nothing could be more boring than being shown a lot of things you don't want to see—with remarkable tact and charm.

NIGEL

I'm glad you think so. I do too.

JORDAN

But I wonder how far you really believe in the Crown, Nigel. For instance, you called the members of the Royal Family the most popular figures in the country.

NIGEL

And so they are.

JORDAN

But surely if we really believed in the Crown, we wouldn't think about royalty in this way at all. They're not competing for popularity, are they? They're not entertainers, film stars, television personalities—God help us all! Can you imagine yourself, as a subject of Elizabeth the First, telling me that Her Majesty was one of the most popular figures in the country? Or congratulating her on her most recent provincial tour? It's unthinkable.

NIGEL

Of course. But ours is a different kind of a monarchy.

JORDAN

But I ask myself if, today, it's any kind of a monarchy worth calling one. Now there are one or two quite sound arguments for a monarchy, even though it makes anything like social democracy impossible except in small countries. But it offers the nation a continuing symbol of the state, lending itself to every form of impressive pageantry. Instead of a fussy president, who used to play bridge badly at your club, a mere chairman of the board hastily transformed into a father figure, at the head of a monarchical society we have an archetypal figure, the holy child, the culture hero, the fascinating feminine image, or the wise old man. Again, as kings and queens inherit their position and power, instead of grabbing them, there's a chance that some of them may be sensible agreeable persons, unlike party leaders who become corrupted by ambition and power-seeking. It's the man who doesn't want power who should have it. And with a real monarchy such a man may very well succeed to the throne.

NIGEL

Yes, but of course—but with us——

JORDAN

The Crown doesn't rule—exactly——

NIGEL

On the other hand, people feel a loyalty to a king or queen who wouldn't care tuppence about a president. And look what happens in the dominions. I doubt if we could keep the Commonwealth together without the Crown.

JORDAN

So we're always being told. But in this matter the dominions come off better than we do in England. The Canadian or Australian is able to live in a social democracy. But if he wants to put out a flag or two and shout for a queen, he's able to do so while still enjoying his social democracy. Topside doesn't control him; indeed, it flatters him, being afraid of him. But Topside isn't afraid of the English, and all it has to do now is to help them to deceive themselves. And here the Crown's pressed into service.

NIGEL

Are you suggesting that Topside controls the Crown?

JORDAN

The Throne and Court are now the glamour-and-pageantry department of Topside: third floor on the right, past the honours-and-titles department. Now don't look angry, Nigel. No royal personage is about to be insulted. But you must understand that the Crown exists now as part of Topside. Do you remember some screaming big headlines in the popular press, a few years ago? *Come on, Margaret*—that sort of thing? But if the lady's a royal personage, she can't be treated in this fashion; and if she's a private person, then she's entitled to settle her affairs in private. All this reflects the new false view of the Crown, the idea that royal personages belong to the people, just as film stars, television favourites, leading figures in sport, belong to the people. The time-old view, remember, was that the people belonged to the Crown. *Our people*, cried the kings and queens. But now Topside has taken over. And the danger here, Nigel—and it's a danger that haunts all Topside's activities—is the profound difference between appearance and reality. Once again, it's the sinister chameleon-like magic of the polyp that's fed because it looks like a pet dog or a basket of kittens.

NIGEL
What exactly have you in mind?

JORDAN
You want an example? Let's take the Coronation. Now there can never have been a coronation on which so much interest was focused as this last one. Every resource of mass communication was used to create excitement about it. And in the midst of that excitement, solemn leading articles were printed, sermons were preached, headmasters' addresses were delivered, all explaining the deep symbolic value, to us as a nation, of this crowning of a queen. That's true, isn't it?

NIGEL
Yes, that was the great topic——

JORDAN
The master theme. Now at the time I disagreed sharply with many old friends of mine, and made them angry by

telling them that in my opinion the state of the English would be worse and not better after this Coronation. And for this reason—that all the emotion that had been generated couldn't lead to any action. If the queen, immediately after she'd been crowned, could have announced a revolutionary policy of her own, perhaps telling us to stop wasting money on nuclear weapons and to spend some of it trying to make this country look less like a huge dreary slum, then far more good than harm would have been done. The emotion would have produced some action. But nothing happened. There was no reality behind this splendid and exciting appearance. The tremendous emotional build-up was followed only by a let-down. So into the vacuum went feelings of disappointment, disillusion, cynicism. All the leading articles, sermons, addresses, were a waste of paper and air. No increase of patriotism, public spirit, devotion to the national welfare, followed the Coronation. On the contrary, the state of the nation was worse than it had been before.

NIGEL

But people *had* felt something, and they'd enjoyed it all——

JORDAN

As a show. A Topside show for Takers. For what's the reality now behind all this pretended fervent devotion to the Crown, a devotion encouraged by every sycophantic and nauseating device of mass communications, which now ask us to believe that every routine state visit is a marvel of romance and beauty, like the wedding procession at the end of a fairy-tale? What respect can we have for a pageantry that merely divides its returns between the tourist traffic and the power enjoyed by men with striped

[45]

trousers and brief-cases? It's a fake. It's the travel agency's Passion Play on a larger scale. This isn't the fault of the Royal Family. The situation's too strong for them. But now either they're the representatives or the prisoners of Topside—take your choice. Remove the glamour of the monarchy and Topside begins to look nearly as shabby as it is. What we have now are the crown jewels lighting up a rat race.

NIGEL

I take exception to that, sir.

JORDAN

But don't mistake me. The wearers of the jewels don't know it's a rat race. They're just doing what they conceive to be their duty. They don't know they're now working for Topside and so may help to ruin England.

NIGEL

Perhaps they're not working for Topside, after all. Perhaps Topside's working for them.

JORDAN

You can easily test that for yourself, Nigel. The next time you find yourself among some important Topsiders, tell them you've become a genuine royalist. Say that it's been quite obvious ever since Suez that far too much power these days is claimed by the Prime Minister, that we ought to change our constitution, to avoid this concentration of power, that we might try something like the American constitution, but of course substituting the Crown for the Presidency. The monarch then would have real power——

NIGEL

They'd laugh at me, and I'd have asked for it.

JORDAN

Right. Then don't tell me that perhaps Topside's working for the Crown——

NIGEL

I meant as a symbol——

JORDAN

But a symbol of what, these days? If of power—then whose? The Crown hasn't any. The people haven't any, except for an election day every few years. We're back then to Topside. And if Topside actually possesses the power, then let Topside come out into the open and ask us to cheer while it represents itself.

NIGEL

It may all be illogical, like a lot of typically English institutions, but it works.

JORDAN

And I say, it doesn't work, not in the way you think it does. The reason it doesn't is that England's no longer a country of aristocrats with a social hierarchy, a pyramid with the Crown as the apex. England may still look like that from inside Buckingham Palace. It may look like that to the crowd waiting outside Buckingham Palace. But it isn't. You can't see the truth for the glitter. The reality here is Topside, the power system that believes in nothing but itself, and so uses the Crown and doesn't serve it.

Whatever glamour and grace, charm and sense of duty, innocence removed from the dusty intrigues, are still associated with the persons of the monarchy, these become more and more the spoils and trappings of Topside, giving a shabby and cynical scramble for power, when it succeeds, gilt and ermine and fine feathers to dazzle the crowd. Yes, Nigel, and what remains from a vanished age, a residue like a potpourri from great names, selfless deeds, brave hard service for the nation, is fragrantly scattered over men who've arrived at the Top because they believe in nothing but arriving there. So I say, Nigel, either give the Crown some real power, to free it from Topside, to enable its friends and advisers to challenge Topside . . . or remove it and every vestige of its gorgeous paraphernalia, its orders and titles, coronets and robes, banners and guards, so that the citizens of a plain republic can see Topside as it really is.

NIGEL
I can't imagine anything more dreary.

JORDAN
I can. And that is England after ten more years of Topside, a Topside finally triumphant and unchallenged; ten more years of national self-deception, of Topside religion, Topside royalty, Topside politics, Topside culture, Topside journalism; ten more years when originality, inventiveness, and creative enthusiasm will be smothered to death by memoranda and minutes, and the nation's energy will run down for ever. Fifty million dupes living in a slum. Even though you aren't one of the dupes and are making good Topside progress, I don't think you'll find that very gay. England could be great and happy under a

monarch who did more ruling and less appearing. England could be great and happy as a republic. Restoration is one way out, and revolution is another. But Topside, once you see it for what it really is, a power organism that stands for everything and believes in nothing, a huge conspiracy of ambition without talent, you will realise offers the country nothing but decay and ultimate ruin. A people can't be nourished and fortified by a sham. The chameleon polyp will be fed and fed and will grow and grow until it brings the house down. Ten more years of the Big Lie and both those who wear it and those who stare at it will find themselves living in a bargain basement. Have a whisky and soda?

NIGEL

Thank you, sir. Just a small one—for the road.

JORDAN

Say *When* for the whisky, Nigel. And *Where* for the road.

NIGEL

When. Thank you, sir. As for *Where*, England's always come through.

JORDAN

But only when she's stopped deceiving herself. And how can she do that under Topside, which exists to encourage self-deception?

NIGEL

Well, sir, here's hoping you're wrong!

JORDAN

You drink to that. I'll drink to this—to the hope that very soon some of you will stop joining in, will risk confusion, instability, even revolution, to begin taking Topside to pieces.

THE END

PLAYS

Volume I

Dangerous Corner
Johnson Over Jordan
Eden End
Music at Night
Time and the Conways
The Linden Tree
I Have Been Here Before

Volume II

Laburnum Grove
The Golden Fleece
Bees on the Boat Deck
How Are They at Home
When We Are Married
Ever Since Paradise

Volume III

Cornelius
An Inspector Calls ✓
People at Sea
Home is Tomorrow
They Came to a City
Summer Day's Dream

ESSAYS AND AUTOBIOGRAPHY

Delight

Rain Upon Godshill

Midnight on the Desert

All About Ourselves and Other Essays
(chosen by Eric Gillet)

Thoughts in the Wilderness

CRITICISM AND MISCELLANEOUS

Meredith (E.M.L.)

The English Comic Characters

Peacock (E.M.L.)

English Humour (Heritage Series)

Brief Diversions

Postscripts

Journey Down a Rainbow
(with Jacquetta Hawkes)

The Art of the Dramatist

Topside